EIR (ISSN 0273-6314) *is published weekly
(50 issues), by EIR News Service, Inc.,
P.O. Box 17390, Washington, D.C. 20041-0390.
(703) 777-9451*

European Headquarters: E.I.R. GmbH, Postfach
Bahnstrasse 9a, D-65205, Wiesbaden, Germany
Tel: 49-611-73650
Homepage: http://www.eirna.com
e-mail: eirna@eirna.com
Director: Georg Neudecker

Montreal, Canada: 514-461-1557

Denmark: EIR - Danmark, Sankt Knuds Vej 11,
basement left, DK-1903 Frederiksberg, Denmark.
Tel.: +45 35 43 60 40, Fax: +45 35 43 87 57. e-mail:
eirdk@hotmail.com.

Mexico City: EIR, Sor Juana Inés de la Cruz 242-2
Col. Agricultura C.P. 11360
Delegación M. Hidalgo, México D.F.
Tel. (5525) 5318-2301
eirmexico@gmail.com

The Future Lies
In Eurasia

You Have Totally Failed— It's Time to Bow Out

March 17—You who believe it all comes down to numbers. You who believe it all comes down to money (and sex). In one sense, you've finally won it all, especially after almost four terms of George W. Bush and Barack Obama. Now there's probably no school in the country that teaches actual science,— only empty mathematics, the fetishism of numbers,— which is the same old babble of the ancient Babylonian priesthood. And as LaRouche PAC leader Kesha Rogers of Texas has pointed out, when Obama shut down our space program, he shut down the last vestige of the optimistic, capable America of Jack Kennedy which the world rightly looked up to.

You've won,— but you've won what? The United States and the whole trans-Atlantic region is nothing but a corpse now. Unlike the United States of Franklin Roosevelt or Jack Kennedy, the United States of Barack Obama is hated throughout the world as the mass murderer he is, and it is. All we represent now is Obama's threat of death from the skies to the murder victims he selects in the White House every Tuesday, in special meetings called "Terror Tuesdays." And beyond that, Obama's imminent intention of a species-extinguishing thermonuclear attack, especially, right now, against China.

Our economy is gone under Obama, hope is gone, and the strata of our most productive skilled workers are instead committing suicide in unheard-of numbers. Yes, indeed, you've won. But won what?

This the long-delayed payoff for allowing Franklin Roosevelt's policies to be reversed by the FBI beginning in 1944, while that President was still alive, although exhausted, and still in the White House. This is the payoff for allowing Jack Kennedy to be assassinated, and the thrust of his policies with him. For allowing his younger brother to be assassinated within reach of the White House, without the needed fight to continue their legacy. Then, when Ronald Reagan was severely wounded in an assassination attempt at the very beginning of his term, the Bush family used the period of Reagan's long convalescence to substantially take over his Presidency, and railroad Lyndon LaRouche to prison, to bury the revolutionary "SDI" policies LaRouche had authored for Reagan, which would have saved this nation by pivotting into a new Renaissance for mankind.

Where were you then? Where are you now?

Now that you have rejected all these attempts to save you, only a much harsher treatment is still available to you. Finally reject once and for all, every idea that it all comes down to numbers (or sex), and from there, finally grasp Lyndon LaRouche's discovery dating back to the 1950s, which revolutionized the science of economy, analogous to Bernhard Riemann's great scientific discovery displayed in his *Habilitation Dissertation.*

Now this discovery is being reflected back into the dying trans-Atlantic system from a successful Eurasia, especially from Russia, China, and the BRICS nations. Lyndon LaRouche was integrally involved in the fashioning of the unprecedented Russia-China alliance which was at the heart of the RIC that became the BRICS, but that is a longer story for another time. After developing the SDI policy for Reagan, Lyndon LaRouche worked with his wife Helga to develop what became known as the Eurasian Land-Bridge, today called the New Silk Road, or China's "One Belt, One Road" policy, which is at the heart of the Renaissance of Eurasia.

If America is to survive, it must join with China and Russia now. Obviously, national identities and senses of national identity will change. Those who have joined the numbers game must recognize their failure and step down. The rest of us must rise to the level which Lyndon LaRouche has so long represented.

EIR Contents

www.larouchepub.com Volume 43, Number 13, March 25, 2016

Cover This Week

Shanghai, China's largest city, at night

Creative Commons-SA 2.0/Harry Alverson

I. Science as an Existential Moral Question

FACE REALITY

The Trans-Atlantic Is Doomed: The Future of Mankind Lies in Eurasia

March 16—The *Daily Telegraph*'s Ambrose Evans-Pritchard has gone hysterical over his recent "discovery" that the trans-Atlantic region is now entering a hyperinflationary blowout. In fact, anyone in their right mind should be well aware that the United States and Europe are already doomed. The U.S. economy is hopeless, and nothing short of a total shift in policy—away from the belief in money over human creativity—can avoid total destruction. There can be no economic revival or even survival under the present policies. It is a miracle that the United States still even exists at this point, since there are no mechanisms to save the economy.

The crisis is most graphically expressed in the sky-rocketing rates of suicide, drug overdose deaths, and declining life expectancy in the United States.

We are on the edge of a global collapse, from which the trans-Atlantic region cannot possibly survive. The Crash can come any day at this point, and it is this reality that has prompted the hysteria from the likes of European Central Bank (ECB) head Mario Draghi and British Crown scribbler Evans-Pritchard.

The only recourse for the trans-Atlantic region is to cancel Wall Street and London—wipe them out altogether, and then completely change the concept of the economic system.

There are two irreconcilable concepts of economy. There is the British-Wall Street concept of money, money, money. Money *per se* has nothing to do with real value. The alternative system, the Hamiltonian System that FDR understood and carried out, rejects

Theo Pirard

China's first female astronaut, Liu Yang, gave a powerful interview after the National People's Congress on the prospects for China's space program. Here she is shown (right) with EIR's William Jones and Marsha Freeman at the Naples International Astronautical Congress in 2012.

Xinhua/Xing Guangli

Chinese Premier Li Keqiang made it clear at the National People's Congress that no outside political force was going to disrupt the China-Russia strategic partnership. Premier Li Keqiang is shown here greeting journalists at his press conference after the closing of the Congress on March 16.

money, rejects Wall Street. It is based on human discoveries that translate into scientific and technological advances that create real wealth and advance mankind's growth.

President Franklin Delano Roosevelt had the concepts, and put those concepts into practice as President—until the FBI and the Republicans shut down the Roosevelt program even before FDR's untimely death. No system built on money and finance can work, and that was what FDR understood.

Russian President Vladimir Putin does not operate in a money system. The Chinese leadership under Xi Jinping do not operate in a money system. Eurasia is being organized under different principles, led by China's quest to realize man's extraterrestrial imperative. This idea was available for all to see on the final day of the just-concluded National People's Congress in Beijing. One of the PLA delegates, China's first female astronaut, Liu Yang, gave a powerful interview to CCTV on the prospects of China's space program. China is also well underway in constructing the world's first commercial high-temperature gas-cooled reactor. This is real economy—not the insanity of money, money, money that has plagued the United States since the death of FDR, with very few moments of exception.

In a different way, Russian President Putin personifies the same principle: The key to everything that

Putin has done to turn around the Syrian situation, is that he is always on the move, always pulling off a surprise flank—at the strategic level. Putin is well aware that he is not acting alone, but is operating on behalf of a partnership with China. Chinese Premier Li Keqiang made this point clear in his final address to the NPC: No third party factor is going to disrupt the China-Russia strategic partnership. In India, Prime Minister Modi has launched a revolution in the agricultural sector, which is key to India's future. In his new budget, he announced an 84% increase in investment in the agricultural sector—on top of related investments in roads, rails, chemicals, and fertilizer production.

Putin is driven by a deep personal experience. Much of his family died during the Nazi invasion of the Soviet Union in World War II. That experience informs his mind. Without an appreciation of who Putin is as a world leader, and where he came from, it is impossible to understand his actions. That is why the vast majority of so-called "strategists" in the West are baffled by his flanking actions.

The Importance of Riemann For Our Future

by Bruce Director

March 20—In the summer of 1854, a twenty-eight year old aspiring professor stood before the mathematics faculty of Göttingen University, to deliver the lecture required to habilitate into their ranks.[1] Unlike on most such occasions, where the aspirant seeks to impress upon the assembled his ability to present the subject matter in a manner consistent with prevailing standards, Bernhard Riemann told the conclave that they, like those similarly situated for the past two thousand years, were horribly mistaken. They had missed the obvious. Their approach toward science was wrong. He situated his polemic in the domain of geometry, but his point was much broader, aimed at overthrowing a debilitating flaw in scientific method that had infected every field, and was hindering the prospects for future progress. Specifically, he insisted that scientists had accepted certain precepts and axioms as the foundations of geometry without ever inquiring into whether these foundations were even true. Consequently, he told them, all they believed could be, and most likely is, wrong. And further, that there was nothing they could do to rectify their state of self-deluded ignorance, unless they abandoned their department of mathematics altogether, and joined with him in the

Carl Friedrich Gauss (1777-1855)

quest for real knowledge.

In this lecture, as well as in the wide-ranging output of his all-too-short creative life, Riemann ignited a revolution that paved the way for all progress in science since. He forced science to recognize that the generation of concepts comes before calculation, and that only a rigorous examination of the workings of the creative mind, not logic or mathematics, can provide a secure foundation for progress in Man's understanding and mastery in, and over, the universe. Progress in science depends on digging up and clearing away the false, but unquestioned underlying assumptions, that prejudice our thoughts and hinder our ability to create entirely new ideas.

However, with few exceptions, most notably Riemann's teacher, Carl Friedrich Gauss, Albert Einstein, and Lyndon LaRouche, Riemann's ideas have either been attacked or, at best, grudgingly acknowledged and ignored. Instead, science, especially since the ascendancy of Bertrand Russell's logical reductionism at the beginning of the Twentieth Century, has been shackled in a tangle of mathematical rules that chain thought to the very axioms and assumptions that must be broken. The conflict that has raged over the past 165 years concerning Riemann's method touches on all the essential struggles that mankind has faced in the intervening period, and that confront us today. Thus, LaRouche is entirely

---

1. Bernhard Riemann, "On the Hypotheses which Lie at the Foundation of Geometry" (1854) in English translation.

justified, and prescient, in raising, once again, the significance of Riemann's thought in this present period.

Essential Features of Riemann's Thought

To fully grasp this meaning would require a thorough and exhaustive study of Riemann's corpus, which is beyond our scope here. Nevertheless it is possible, in this short space, to acquaint the reader with the core of the issue by touching upon some of the essential features of his contributions.

The habilitation lecture is a good place to start. Riemann had come to Göttingen several years earlier, intending to study theology, being the descendant of several generations of Lutheran ministers. Shortly after arriving, he switched his attention to science, having been recruited by Gauss, who recognized in Riemann a creative spark rare among his other students. Gauss, already an old man by the time of Riemann's arrival, had himself generated a plethora of revolutions in science. But during most of his career he labored in the climate of enforced pessimism that dominated Europe in the period following the oligarchical reaction against the Leibnizian spirit of the American Revolution.

Absurdity of Euclidean Geometry

As a result, though Gauss was justly famous for many astounding scientific breakthroughs, such as his discovery of the orbit of Ceres, and new discoveries of the nature of gravity and electromagnetism, he kept much of his deep thinking on the fundamentals of science to himself. Very dear to his heart were his insights into the characteristic flaw of mathematics—that the true nature of the universe, and man's role in it, cannot be discovered by mathematical formulas or deductive logic.

This failing infected all science. Instead, Gauss recognized that the subject of science was the interaction of the creative powers of the human mind with the

Wikimedia Commons
Georg Friedrich Bernhard Riemann (1826-1866), a student of Gauss.

physical universe, which created new concepts and new states of existence.

Exemplary of this are Gauss's insights into the complete absurdity of what has become known as Euclidean geometry. The acceptance of Euclidean geometry as physically real, had been the dominant thought in physics and mathematics, but also more generally. The oligarchy's favorite philosopher at the time, Immanuel Kant, had insisted that Euclidean geometry must be true because it was the only geometry the mind was capable of conceiving that was consistent with sense perception.

Gauss, like LaRouche many years later, found this standpoint to be absurd, and mind-deadening. In his earliest private writings, Gauss noted that all the results of Euclidean geometry were derived by a deductive progression from an unproven, and unprovable, axiom of parallel lines. Similarly, Gauss delighted in pointing out that something as simple as the distinction between right and left, could never be decided by mathematical procedure, but required a reference to a physical effect. Although Gauss's notebooks are filled with discussions about the stupidity of accepting Euclidean geometry as true, he never dared to state this publicly. On numerous occasions, Gauss told his closest friends that he could never publish his thoughts in his lifetime, for fear of backlash.

Riemann's Habilitation Lecture

It is not hard to imagine the delight of the 78-year old Gauss, when his young protégé, Riemann, approached him for advice on what subject to present for his habilitation lecture. Riemann presented his mentor with a choice of three subjects, the last of which was on the foundations of geometry. Gauss insisted that Riemann make this his subject.

It is also not hard to imagine, and eyewitness accounts confirm it, that the normally dour Gauss was vis-

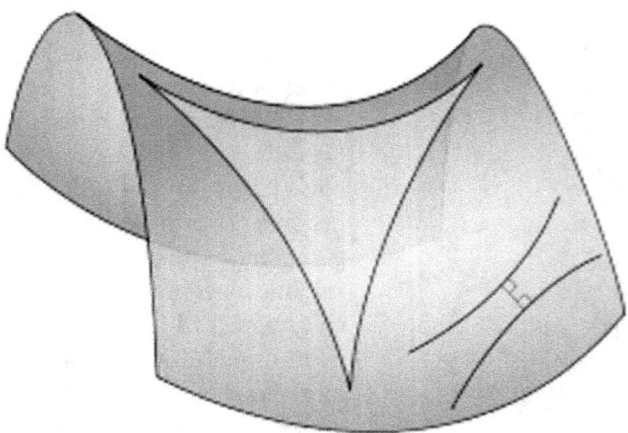

Tad Boniecki/soler7.com

Were you taught that the sum of the angles of a triangle must always be 180 degrees?

ibly delighted when Riemann opened his lecture:

> It is known that geometry assumes, both the notion of space and the first principles of constructions in space, as given in advance. She gives definitions of them which are merely nominal, while the true determinations appear in the form of axioms. The relation of these assumptions remains, consequently, in darkness; we perceive neither whether, and how far, their connection is necessary, nor *à priori*, whether it is possible.
>
> From Euclid to Legendre (to name the most famous of modern reforming geometers) this darkness was cleared up neither by mathematicians nor by such philosophers as concerned themselves with it. The reason of this is doubtless that the general notion of multiply extended magnitudes (in which space-magnitudes are included) remained entirely unworked. I have in the first place, therefore, set myself the task of constructing the notion of a multiply extended magnitude out of general notions of quantity. It will follow from this that a multiply extended magnitude is capable of different measure-relations, and consequently that space is only a particular case of a triply extended magnitude. But it then follows as a necessary consequence that the propositions of geometry cannot be derived from general notions of magnitude, but that the properties which distinguish space from other conceivable triply extended magnitudes are only to be deduced from experience. Thus arises the

problem, to discover the simplest matters of fact from which the measure-relations of space may be determined; a problem which from the nature of the case is not completely determinate, since there may be several systems of matters of fact which suffice to determine the measure-relations of space—the most important system for our present purpose being that which Euclid has laid down as a foundation. These matters of fact are—like all matters of fact—not necessary, but only of empirical certainty; they are hypotheses. We may therefore investigate their probability, which within the limits of observation is of course very great, and inquire about the justice of their extension beyond the limits of observation, on the side both of the infinitely great and of the infinitely small.

Riemann then went on to outline the basic means to replace the mathematical fantasy-geometry of Euclid with a real physical one. In such a case, assumptions, such as the number of dimensions, the curvature, or the discreteness or continuity of space, are no longer given by *à priori* assumptions, but only determined by real physical investigation. To do this, Riemann insisted, one must reject the dogma that Euclidean geometry must be true because it is consistent with sense perception. As Riemann noted in the above-cited excerpt from his lecture, it is only when science reaches beyond the domain of sense perception, that real physics begins.

This pursuit would eventually become the basis for Einstein's and Planck's discoveries in atomic physics, as well as Einstein's theories of special and general relativity. It is beyond our scope here to delve more deeply into the rich field of ideas contained in Riemann's short lecture, but suffice it to say that Riemann's concluding admonition, "This leads us into the domain of another science, that of physics, into which the object of today's proceedings does not allow us to enter," gave Gauss great delight, and left many of the other participants stewing.

Science Reaches Beyond Sense Perception

The approach to geometry expressed in Riemann's habilitation lecture was preceded, and followed, by its application to many areas of science including gravity, electromagnetism, light, hydrodynamics, thermodynamics, and physiology. In all cases Riemann focused on the contradiction that arose between the behavior of physical phenomena, and the prevailing mathematical concepts which were largely based on the relationships that seem obvious from the standpoint of sense perception.

Like Plato, Kepler, and Leibniz before him, Riemann understood that sense perception is only a shadow of reality, even in domains accessible to the senses, let alone in the very large and very small. This is obviously the case in investigations concerning non-perceptible phenomena such as gravity, light, electromagnetism, and heat, which cannot be perceived directly.

Riemann focused on the creation of new concepts that advance our understanding of the principles underlying these phenomena, instead of merely describing the observed effects, as when he pioneered what have become known as complex functions.

The Role of the Human Mind

Though this work has been falsely represented as purely mathematical investigation, largely because the history has been written by his enemies, Riemann's development of these ideas is based on his intention to dig deeper into the direct role of the human mind in the universe. Toward what would be the end of his life, he was led to study the interaction of the mind with the physical world by investigating the paradoxes associated with hearing.[2] In his uncompleted study, Riemann poses the contradictions between the simply mechanical concept of sound, pushing and pulling on the hearing organ, and what hearing actually does. No mechanical explanation of sound can account for the mind's ability to distinguish subtle changes in, for example, timbre and tone, that are essential to conveying ideas.

And this brings us to what is the unifying quest in Riemann's scientific work most desperately needed today: developing a deeper capacity to grasp the nature of human creativity through its role in the universe.

In 2018 a Chinese spacecraft will land on the far side of the Moon and peer into the universe from a vantage point never before accessed by Man. At that point, everything Man has thought about the nature of space will be brought into question. It will be a triumph for Riemann's thought. Its prospect reminds us why we urgently need a new appreciation of Riemann today.

---

2. Bernhard Riemann, "The Mechanism of the Ear" (1866) in English translation, *Fusion*, Sept.-Oct. 1984, p. 31.

The Space Program and True Economic Value

by Kesha Rogers

The following statement was delivered on the La-Rouche PAC International Webcast of March 18.

I would like to start by continuing to develop what has been and must be the focal point by which we come to understand the necessity for the revival and the defense, not just of the U.S. space program, which I have continued to be a leader in championing, but of the necessity and development of what our space program truly represents for the progress of all mankind. As I stated in a recent *EIR* editorial, to understand the space program, one must go beyond the standpoint of looking at the economic conditions of the United States, or some practical applications to economics where the space program will provide benefits.

We also have to look at the space program from the standpoint that it represents the true conception of real economic value. This is what is actually missing from our thinking. What has been attacked by the current Wall Street/British imperial system is that economic value is based, from their standpoint, on monetary value, and not on the creative powers and progress of the human mind.

EIRNS/Stephanie Nelson

We have to look at the space program as a true expression of real economic value. It's much more than a matter of practical economic applications. Kesha Rogers is pictured here as a candidate for Congress in 2010, at the Lincoln Dinner in Houston.

The Identity and Purpose of Mankind

The real question at hand right now is to bring about a new conception of what is the identity and what is the purpose of mankind. I have continued to use the example and the works of the great pioneer of space flight, Krafft Ehricke. It is his conception of mankind as a space-faring creature with an "extra-terrestrial imperative" that must be identified and understood.

Take the example of what China is doing now. It is completely rejecting the monetarist policy. The space program is not based on considerations of how much money you're going to put into pet projects and specific projects. It is creating something that has never been

created before, to actually create a new conception and a new identity for mankind, from the standpoint of the idea of acting on the future. That is what is being developed, for instance, by China in its investigation of the far side of the Moon.

People may look at this and say, "Well how is this going to benefit us? How is this going to improve economic conditions, in terms of monetary value, for any of us?" That is the wrong way to look at it. You have seen two opposing conceptions of mankind. One is coming from the trans-Atlantic system, coming from a collapsing imperial system that has been based on money and monetary value, a system that is dying, and the other is represented by what Russia and China are doing. What I have developed in my recent writing is that the latter approach was also the thinking of the great leaders of our nation, represented by the ideas of Alexander Hamilton, Abraham Lincoln, Franklin Roosevelt, and John F. Kennedy. They were not focused just on creating new projects, per se, but on a new and different conception of the identity of mankind.

Take the example of what we in the United States accomplished in landing a man on the Moon—the idea that Kennedy put forward, that by the end of the decade of the 1960s we would land a man on the Moon and return him safely to Earth. What was the vision and intention behind that? Was it just the idea that we would go and plant our flag on the Moon—for some short-term gratification? Or was it a forward-thinking outlook, in terms of the direction of mankind, recognizing what space pioneer Ehricke understood—that mankind is not just a creature of planet Earth. We are not just a part of, as he called it, a "closed system." So it is our responsibility to go out do what no other animal is capable of doing, of actually conquering and developing—coming to understand the purpose of mankind and accomplishing the development of mankind in the Universe as a creature of our Solar System and our Galaxy.

The Renaissance Ideal

Ehricke was very insightful in writing about the Renaissance, the Italian Renaissance, as an achievement of human progress. He argued that that Classical Renaissance contributed to the development of what centuries later became our space program, and provided the intention that guided the direction of space travel and the space program.

Ehricke wrote, "The development of the idea of space travel was always the most logical and most noble consequence of the Renaissance ideal, which again placed man in an organic and active relationship with his surrounding universe and which perceived in the synthesis of knowledge and capabilities its highest ideals."

Look at this from the standpoint of Ehricke's understanding that the Renaissance was guided by the scientific breakthroughs of a Brunelleschi or the breakthroughs that came about from the works of Kepler—that the idea of mankind is to create something fundamentally new, something that has never been created before and, in so doing, to increase the relationship of mankind to the Universe.

Now that's economic value! That is precisely what is not being discussed in the debates back and forth from the standpoint of members of Congress addressing the space community on which budgets should be cut and which should not. As I stated before, we have to have, in defense of the space program, a new conception of the direction of mankind. That means we are

Moon landing, 1969: "One small step for a man, one giant leap for mankind." We must create a new identity for mankind from the standpoint that we act on the future.

removing all limitations on progress, all limitations imposed on mankind's ability to continue to understand how to make new discoveries of the scientific principles of what's out there. Why should we actually investigate the Solar System? What is our mission in doing so? It is not about a money-making, short-term gratification.

So I think this emphasis that Ehricke put on the Renaissance as an ideal, of looking at why we have, as a human species, an extraterrestrial imperative, is really continued in what you're seeing coming from China, not just in its space program, but in the development of the win-win strategy of cooperation for all mankind—for all nations to come together to address the necessary challenges of the economic condition of the planet by actually recognizing that the solutions do not lie right here on planet Earth.

That is the conception I want to get across. I hope to have further discussion, as we continue this fight, to identify what is the real mission of the space program, and how we might rid the world immediately of this current dead system that is keeping us from advancing in the way that we should.

We Have To Fight to Establish in People A Loyalty to Creating the Kind of Behavior that Makes Life Worth Living

The following excerpts are taken from the March 17 LaRouche PAC Fireside Chat and the March 19 LaRouche PAC Manhattan Town Hall Meeting.

Question: I was talking to a couple, and I presented them with the New Silk Road, NASA, and other items that we're doing, and tried to explain to them that we're not backing a specific candidate. They're a bunch of losers. But they still asked me, after I told them, they said, "well, that's good, but who are you back as candidate?"

What I'm saying is, some of these people are so hard-wired to this election thing—and it's difficult to get past that. Is there any tactic that I'm missing here?

LaRouche: The whole world, the United States, Europe, are now in the process of the greatest crisis in all modern history, probably. It's a fair estimation, because the implications of the dangers which exist now, at these times under these conditions, are something which is unprecedented in modern history, specifically modern history. And therefore, we have to act on something not which we worry about, but something which we know how to do something about. If you don't know what to do to fix the problem, just don't talk. Let other voices speak. Now, the point here is, there are several points. People don't understand what humanity is. They believe that babies come and go, and that babies die, and people go, and

that it's just a sequel of events, of birth and death, and something in between.

The fact of the matter is the important thing is to mobilize people who are qualified, in the matter of science, the practice of science, and its progress. Without that ability, without that facility, to forecast the future of mankind on that basis, society is, as the case of the United States today demonstrates, a garbage dump! It has no intrinsic value in its present operation. Similar things are true in Europe.

Less so in Russia; Russia has better conditions, China has better conditions, other nations in that area have better conditions. Egypt, for example, has better conditions. So why are we saying this, that at some

Albert Duce/CCBY-SA 3.0

All the jobs are gone. How do we move beyond words and actually solve the problem? Here, the western part of the abandoned Packard Automotive Plant in Detroit, Michigan, in 2009.

time, something is going to come miraculously to save you? It's you that must save yourself by getting rid of the habits that you've allowed yourself to adopt. That's the way to approach it.

Question: I am from the poisoned-water capital of the United States, Flint, Michigan. It may be a shock for people to find out there is only one auto plant that I know of left today in Flint, the truck and bus operation on Van Slyke Road, and they don't make from start to finish; the doors, the fenders, and the frames are brought into Flint, because we do not have a manufacturing capability here in Flint any more. The TPP and Carter's deal pushed all the manufacturing jobs away.

Lyndon LaRouche and his team talk about the Silk Road, I hear about it all the time. Years ago, America could already have had the Silk Road, but instead we had the Bushes and their families, the criminals, the Clintons, and Obama's team. My question is, how do we move beyond words, and actually solve the problem?

LaRouche: What we need to do, what we're going to have to do, is first of all, get a new President. That's absolutely essential. The lessons of what Franklin Roosevelt did as President gives you an example, a model of the way in which you can approach this question of problems. If you look back to what happened in the time of Franklin Roosevelt's inauguration, in that period, that's exactly what happened. It happened! Why did it happen? It happened because Franklin Roosevelt, as a leader of the Presidency of the United States at that time, moved everything, in places in which most of the people out there were totally unemployed—like even the people in that group you were referring to, right? They were desperately unemployed. They were abused in the highest degree of abuse.

And Franklin Roosevelt and his effort, with great difficulty, moved improvements in the conditions of life of the so-called "working people" of the United States. And turned the United States from this kind of despair, into the most advanced form of industrial and related production in the planet as a whole.

The United States, under Franklin Roosevelt was the great leader of the world. And it's only when he lost

Roosevelt, with great difficulty, brought improvements for working people. Here he signs into law the Social Security Act of 1935, providing unemployment benefits, old age pensions, and welfare benefits for the poorest. Labor Secretary Frances Perkins, who drafted the Act, is directly behind him.

power and was dumped, that we lost the United States. So that's the issue. You don't have to find a new model. The model lies in the kind of intention, which scientists working under the Franklin Roosevelt leadership used to do what was previously considered as the impossible. By 1936, Roosevelt had already established the beginning of his great economic achievement.

And what happened? Well, the FBI got in there; since the FBI got into the United States, the FBI has created a junk shop. They don't have any brains; they don't need brains, that's why they're the FBI. And I'll tell you some day what the initials "FBI" really mean. You may find it charming.

Question: Hi Lyn, it's Alvin in New York. Taking into account actions of the three leading nations as it's expressed in: the update of Modi's move for massive investment in agriculture, China of course on space and the New Silk Road, and now a move to put a hold on and grip on hedge-fund speculation, and then, of course, it continues to reverberate that Putin announced on Monday that his intention was never flight-forward, but rather, like MacArthur to win the peace.

My question to you is, can you elaborate more for us on what is the nature of a strategic leadership, a strategic thinker, how that operates, so that we can try and impart that, first within ourselves, and to a petrified citizenry?

LaRouche: Well, there are several steps you should probably check off as items to be considered in answering such a question. The question can be answered, and it's efficient. It may not be perfect in detail, but it gives you a pretty good picture of what is possible. And you can work out the rest for yourselves. Do your own self-education.

The issue here is that mankind is not what most people call "mankind." That is, the education system, for children for example, and adults in the case of the United States, the teaching in those institutions is a farce, and should be discontinued in favor of a competent form of education. That's a good beginning.

Now, you look at skills, you look at opinions, and you find that these so-called skills are not skills, they're failures. That the popular opinions are absurdities which lead to disasters.

China, with its program for the far side of the Moon, is the leader in space exploration. Here, Earth as seen from the Moon in a photo taken from Apollo 8, 1968.

And we have to go back again, for example, to the Franklin Roosevelt example. President Franklin Roosevelt led the launching of a method of approach, for the United States and its people, which was excellent, and remains in its principle, excellent! So why don't we just go back to that? I know enough about that to know how that can be done. So if they don't agree with me, well, let's get some new people, who do understand what I'm talking about.

The Trans-Atlantic World is Doomed

Question: I think the aspect you're bringing forward about FDR should be the model for us today, and I wanted to emphasize that. In trying to figure out Putin's role in this intervention that he's trying to conduct in the Middle East, I think the question is, if you're talking about leadership in ushering in this power of FDR, how do we intensify this power, to communicate this, and actually win, in the context of humanity?

LaRouche: Well, the problem is, let's look at the world as humanity. The leading nation on the planet today, in terms of progress, is China. That's a fact. China is first of all, not only the most productive rate of improved development of all nations known to us; the British are, of course, just sick, sick people. France is a

disgusting place. The Spanish economy is a disaster. Italy has become a disaster.

Now Putin has made his own role in this thing; he's made a very significant contribution, in which he has depended to a significant degree on the influence of China, because China is the biggest element of progress, in terms of all human development so far.

The United States has become a disaster in terms of policy, in terms of economic design. You see that in the people of the United States. Each generation of people, of all categories, each generation with the exception of the swindlers who steal the money, the United States is degenerating. All of South America is rapidly degenerating, per capita, throughout the territory! And the British are key in organizing this.

So you're talking about a revolution. But a defined revolution: A certain part of the planet works, today, that is Eurasia. It's not all of Eurasia, but the great part of Eurasia. That's the leading part of progress for mankind today. China is developing the program of the back side of the Moon.

So you're living in a period where the United States and the Americas are doomed regions of the world! They're in decline, at an accelerating rate!

Now, that is not necessarily the result. But that requires that we change our ways, that we get rid of the

President, we get rid of the Vice President, we get rid of many of the people in his term of office; throw 'em out! Because they are the ones who are acting out the worsening destruction of the conditions of life of the people of the United States themselves. And that application, that measure, is the one that's applicable.

Through most of the world today, only Russia and China and a few other odd places, have any validity for their form of existence now. The rest of them are all dying, or just plain rotting away. We have to get the people of the world to stop being stupid about this, and look up with their eyes at what the world really is, and make a decision: Get rid of Obama, just to begin with. And get rid of the British Monarchy.

Do that. And then you will find a number of things that can be done, which were improvements. And you will come to realize how important those changes are.

Question: Hi, Mr. LaRouche. How do you see things changing domestically in the financial services realm? Do you ever see us getting away from the Federal Reserve? How will this impact our future, and how we think of currency?

LaRouche: There's not much of a problem here, at all. The problem is, that we have to develop an insight into what a human being is, so that the whole question of the kind of things we've been talking about just during these few hours right now, is exactly that: What is it, that makes mankind qualified to be mankind? As opposed to failures? Now, we know what failures are: Obama's a failure. He's not a decent human being. He's an evil man, and he should be thrown out of office, period. That's a fact.

We have other people in other parts of the planet, it's full of people! The whole British oligarchy are a bunch of thieves, a bunch of degenerates. We have in other parts of Europe, whole packs of people are degenerates. That is, they're of Satanic wont, is a fair description of it.

So we have to fight against this stuff. And that's necessary. Now, we don't try to kill people; we do like to embarrass them when they do bad things. And if we embarrass them sufficiently, they will crawl back into their hole someplace and maybe they'll even improve themselves. That's the way it goes.

That's what it is. There is a standard, a global standard, which should be measured in physical economic terms, which determines what the good society is today. It's maybe not the best society that ever existed, but it's a good society, because it has characteristics which are good for mankind. And that's the way to look at it.

We have to fight to establish in people a loyalty to creating the kind of behavior that makes life worth living. Essentially that's a simple way of putting it. And that's what we have to do. We have to do it for ourselves, we have to do it for other nations, for other people. When you see an injustice being done, you try to intervene and prevent it from being continued. If you see the possibility of neglect, which has the same effect, you want to correct that error.

Question: Hello, Mr. LaRouche. My question tonight has to do with the necessary change in the United States. It's very clear that the population of the United States has gone down the same path as that of the 1939 German population in terms of moral degeneration. Mass murder and such are simply accepted as the nature of how things are, with fumbled, desperate excuses to justify it.

I understand that to change the situation in the United States in the most effective way, is to get various institutions to move quickly on the disposal of Obama, and on action on various programs in place to eliminate the British system and begin the rebuilding process, joining with the Asian orientation. My question generally is, how do citizens drive this process? And how does the Manhattan Project play into this?

LaRouche: Well, it's partly simple in a sense, a simple beginning, when you give up caving in to things that you should realize are not what you really want to do. I mean, you go out and you do things. You go out and have parties and other behavior, and you realize that this is not doing anything good for you, for your family, and your immediate circles. And that's the beginning. It always has been the beginning, when people begin to move in a direction like this, they say, "This was a mistake. This was rotten, this stunk. I'm quitting. Let's go change and do it in a different way." And I've seen that. I've watched it. It does happen. It does not happen enough. . . .

The problem is, that the world as a whole has been drawn, through the influence of the British Empire, has been drawn down deep. In the course of time, nations have come back, step by step. China has become a dominant leader in the progress of mankind. You see what's happened in Egypt, the improvement in Egypt; you see the struggles to do it.

You see how European nations are degenerating, in the main. The United States is degenerating at a rapid rate, at the same time. What're we doing about it? Isn't the problem lying somewhere inside the citizens of these nations? Can we blame this on that, or this, or that? Are these nations themselves not the source of their own disaster?

I would say, "yes." And I'm pretty much of an expert on this subject. The sufferings of the people of the United States are largely, and chiefly, a product of the behavior of the government of the United States, and of the Presidents generally, with some exceptions.

BalkanEU.com

You see the improvement in Egypt; you see the struggles to do it. Here, a portion of the new Suez Canal in 2015.

Question: Hi, I'm an activist here in Los Angeles. I have a question. I'm curious to know what you think of this. I'm in the mental health field by profession and I have seen this pattern, after studying political science and different things like this, including the ongoing pattern of this constant playing of mankind by this empire type of situation. And I've had my own theories about it basically, but what do you honestly think is the problem? Why has man never really able to get this yoke off from around his neck? What do you think the problem is?

LaRouche: All I can say is, that from my experience, that I've seen—I've lived through almost a century, I've seen a lot of these kinds of things, and I've seen in the main, I would say, go back to the beginning of the Twentieth Century. What happened? Bertrand Russell invaded the United States. And Bertrand Russell spread a form of evil.

I mean, for example, scientific people, in terms of their training and skills, in the last century began to become degenerates. Scientists became degenerates, and leading scientists were actually degenerates, based on this kind of influence which was spread to them, through Bertrand Russell, and under the influence of Bertrand Russell. Whereas great people, great and accomplished scientists, were being mocked and ridiculed at the same time. And children were being advised in the process of their maturation to become effectively degenerate.

Most of the education in the schools today, including the graduate schools, general educational schools, are degenerate. Actually the practice of teaching has become largely, increasingly degeneracy, and it's this degeneracy which is a co-factor of the increase of the further degeneracy in the population as a whole, and of the economy of the nation as a whole. These are the issues that have to be considered.

But we have to understand, it's history. And the key thing to this is, Bertrand Russell. What's the meaning of Bertrand Russell? Well, Bertrand Russell was British. That's pretty British; that's pretty evil. He was evil. He remains evil. They haven't been able to bury him enough. And then, what's happened? You have the whole history of science since the Nineteenth Century. After the process of the Nineteenth Century there was a plummeting degeneration of science in the United States, beginning with the Twentieth Century.

And this is what's happened. And thus, we make our own destruction, by consenting to degeneracy. We want to be popular! Why did these scientists who became degenerates, from the Twentieth Century on, why did they become degenerates? Because they wanted to be popular! What causes most people to become degenerates? They want to be popular! They go out and say, "Oh yes, I agree with you! Yes, I agree with you. Yes, I agree with you! Oh, you're very smart, aren't you? Good, I want some money from you." [laughs] Something like that goes on, right? And that's what happens to us.

And the problem is, members of our own society tend to degenerate, because they would like to become successful; they would like become popular; they would like to have a little more money, or a little special sex on the side, where the wife or husband didn't know what was going on; things like that. And that's the way the world has run in large degree.

So you can't complain just by saying flatly, "Oh we have a big problem over here." Well, why did we have a big problem? Because some people went along with the habit; they picked up the habit. You know, you had this thing in the post-World War II period, you had a period of degeneracy throughout the United States, throughout everybody. And it got worse. And this occurred despite the fact of what Franklin Roosevelt had done.

And most of the scientists, so-called, were worse degenerates as they went along. People who were leading scientists in that period, they were the degenerates! They sold their soul, and they had no understanding of science. So, as scientists they were failures. Go through the list of the scientists in that period, going into the Twentieth Century, beyond the Twentieth Century.

And going into the school systems in California, in Massachusetts, for example. All these areas were products of degeneracy because they teach children things which are not true, frauds; they impose behavior which is fraudulent, degenerate. And that's what the problem is.

But! Those who are called the degenerates by me are the worst of them all. And that's the problem. You're going to have to get rid of degeneracy, not by violence, but by shaming people into coming out of the evil practices they indulge in.

It's better to cook the food, than rot it.

From Manhattan

Question: Hi, Lyn, it's A— in New York. I'd like to know more about the understanding of how a real strategic mind like Putin operates, because our population,—we, not the population—we need to understand that better because there's the miracle that was created, and we need to create the same thing here now in the United States.

LaRouche: This is a little bit complicated, because you cannot make a short statement on the answer, a very important answer, to this question. Now, the essential thing is not what happened, in those facts, but goes deeper. And unless you go into those deeper mat-

ters, you do not get a correct estimation of what the implications are of this subject-matter.

What has happened is that the United States and Europe, in general, have now reached a point of self-destruction or a point of termination of the trans-Atlantic community. Because the problem now is, instead of trying to take guesses on what might be factors, you've got to look at the whole picture as a whole. Otherwise you don't get a picture. The picture is that the United States under the leadership of Great Britain, the British system, the dominating role of the British system, especially during the Twentieth Century and beyond, the point is reached now in which the conditions are those of *total collapse* in the trans-Atlantic community inside the trans-Atlantic community! Western Europe, Central Europe, and West of that.

And history has moved to the point of Russia and China, and elements in the picture which fit also in that same set. This includes various relevant parts of Asia. So this is something which is absolutely new.

The problem we face now is that the United States and Western Europe, in particular, are already doomed. That is, in their present situation, in their current practices, they are doomed. Only if we make a transformation within the United States, to overturn the present system of the United States, economic system, then we can get out of this thing. Otherwise, what is happening is that everything is collapsing west of the Atlantic Ocean, everything. And unless we, in the United States, come to a recognition of these hard facts—these are not temptations, these are not simple things—these are hard facts: It means that you have to throw the current President of the United States out of the window, or something like that. If you don't overturn the present system of the United States, and the practices which dominate the present system of the United States, economic practices, then you are looking at chaos. And the included result will be that Asia would be the only significantly surviving area, for any hope of mankind.

In other words, what's happened is the British Empire, which has dominated the whole system, all these years, is now doomed in its present form, its present practices. Only if we can come to an arrangement which throws Obama to Hell, perhaps, or something like that, unless you can do that, you are now actually in a situation where a threat is general thermonuclear war. Unless Obama is thrown out of office, in particular, the threat of a general thermonuclear war is an immediate one. And this is not a joke of any kind; this is not "something bad." This is the threat of extermination. Therefore, we have to understand the fact that this is the case, and that we in the United States have a responsibility to mobilize ourselves to make sure the appropriate response is delivered.

A Legally Organized Coup

Question: I had a chance to spend some time with a senior scientific figure over at the Institute of Advanced Studies, and he had some reactions, and I'd like to hear if you have any reactions to his reactions. He's very much concerned about nuclear war. He's made the point—he comes out of the World War II era himself—and he thinks there's a complete lack of recognition of the threat of nuclear war....

Now I think it's also worth noting that the person we were talking to was very struck by the increase in the mortality rates amongst youth in New York State, as shown by a study that was done concerning New York State and elsewhere. And he fully recognizes the situation in the United States. He may not agree with us on everything. He was very interested in the Eurasian Land-Bridge, he said, "I'm sympathetic."

LaRouche: This is a decision which has to be made. If the people in the United States presently, if leading people in the United States, will clean out the Congress of the bums and the swine, get rid of that, and just revolt against everything that Obama and these bums represent, that is the only way we can protect the people of the United States. That can work.

A coup, organized legally among the membership of the Congress and the institutions attached to that can save the United States from a threat which is now oncoming at an accelerating rate, which can be resisted by using new technologies which are available. They will be weak at first, but they can become stronger. The means exist to supply those kinds of technologies.

That would be the only course to suggest the possibility of avoidance of general warfare, including thermonuclear warfare. Otherwise, we're in trouble. We might survive, but the chances are very poor.

Question: Hi, good afternoon, Mr. LaRouche. My question is regarding what's going to come in the elections this year, after the primaries? I want to have your points about what do you think about this triple challenge, because we have the Democrats on one side; we have the GOP on one side; and we have technically Donald Trump on one side. And how important will the

EIRNS/Stuart Lewis

A coup, organized legally, among the membership of Congress and the institutions attached to it, can save the United States from the oncoming threat. Here, the United States Capitol Building.

Congressional election be?

LaRouche: No, the problem here is, unless we get rid of Obama, from his present position in a short term, we're running out of margin to continue the successful ongoing existence of the United States' organization. In other words, if we do not shut down Obama within a very short period of time, the month of April, for example, if we do not do that, there will be no future for the United States, or much of the world.

The important thing is to throw Obama out of office now as an absolute priority. Get Trump. If we can, get some of the others out. Get rid of these guys because the safety of the United States population depends upon doing exactly that efficiently, now! If you don't understand what I understand—what I know about the facts of the matter, we are running out of the days of toleration of continuation of the present economy of the United States. That's it! We've got to settle it now.

You cannot sit around and wait for a good, happy-happy time to come. You've got to do the kinds of things which help build support for reform, but also conduct the reform at the same time. And in the case of Manhattan, Manhattan is a very important nation in effect in this respect. Because the options for saving the United States from an immediate general collapse are coming on fast. And therefore, if we cannot get some solutions on this thing, the United States population is finished. And it may come in the form of some kind of mass killing, in terms of inside the United States and other kinds of things.

It's already on plan! Inside the United States, the characteristics of the typical members of the formulation of practice of economy is on the edge of actual closing out. We have a short term of opportunity to save this nation from mass destruction of its population.

I've been supporting strongly certain actions in terms of Manhattan and associated Manhattan areas, because Manhattan is such a big, important element in the totality of the U.S. economy, that the health or failure of the United States depends largely on Manhattan. If you understand the economy, that's the picture. And therefore we have to have a policy to defend Manhattan as a part of defending the United States! And what's going on in Texas right now, with the reopening of the space program, is another key factor in this thing.

Don't gamble on wild guesses. These matters are matters which are important. We can deal with them with a certain degree of solemnity. We can do things. We may be able to succeed, we will try to succeed. We're going to try with the help of what the space program has done. A renewed space program has been set into motion in Texas, where the space program was originated for the United States.

We have an option, thereby, in which to build something to save the United States itself. Right now, we're in deep trouble. We're on the edge of doom! We've got to keep the doom away from the door, we've got to find the right programs, which will stimulate some protection for the people of the United States, to rebuild their optimism which they've lost, and to get the bums out, like Obama! And guess who else?

Ching/Creative Commons

Manhattan is such an important element of the U.S. economy that the health or failure of the United States depends largely on Manhattan. We have to have a policy to defend Manhattan as a part of defending the United States! Here, Manhattan's Carnegie Hall in 2013.

Question: I wanted to give you a report on what we've been doing in the work in Brooklyn, to build for the *Messiah* concert on Easter Sunday, at the Visitation Church there.

Actually we've had a very electrified response from the population around the church, but also in response to this *Messiah* program we did in December last year. We're becoming an institution in this area. And it has a lot to do with this Italian principle.

But the concept is that it's a self-organizing process also, on top of what we're doing, to where you now have a very clear understanding, and in fact, as we're handing out the leaflets, you get people who say: "Oh, this is the Schiller Institute!" almost immediately.

And this is the question of the Brooklyn/Manhattan Project that we're creating. We're also getting a lot of musicians who have given up—they haven't really necessarily given up, but they're not in the profession of what they were trained to be musicians in, and they're all working at a bakery, or being waitresses, or something.

But as we're telling them that we're having musicians going to the schools to perform for the kids, and also having this whole program going on, these people are getting remoralized, and they're volunteering to go into the schools and do work with us, and are volunteering their information. They actually want to become active with us.

And so, I wanted to see what your thoughts are on this.

LaRouche: In October of 2014, I had completed a plan for going into Manhattan and emphasizing Manhattan as the center of the core of rebuilding the organization of the United States. And recognize that Manhattan was the only area which had the magic power of its own peculiar nature, and out of its history, to actually do that. And so we have done several things, step by step, since that time, since we made that decision, in order to say, we're going to build a process of increasing the efficiency of the organization in Manhattan. The assumption was that by devoting ourselves to several locations on the total territory of the United States, that by working on those areas, which were, shall we say, the most healthy areas in which to pick up for the United States, that would be the solution to prevent the United States itself from collapsing.

And that if we had no such program, no such support for Manhattan, if we just let the old system run rampant, or rabid, shall we say, that we couldn't have a success. Now we've had successes, and what we've

done in terms of promotion of certain musical programs we've selected as being the best instruments, the most efficient instruments, in trying to revive the U.S. economy in terms of the Manhattan region. That, I think, has tended to work.

It has not worked, because it's still in the process of trying to find its way to work. But the more we get this thing, you change the moral characteristic of outlook of people within the Manhattan region, and that sets something forth into motion. And I think that's what you want.

Question: You dropped a couple of political bombshells. What I want to hear more about, frankly, is what you mean by a "legally organized coup," because I really like that idea. I want you to expand on that.

LaRouche: No, the point is, it's necessary for us to understand that we can, by these kinds of means, overthrow an illegal government. The illegal government is Obama. And that is buttressed by Obama's associates and by the people who preceded Obama!

So the time has come that we must actually change the laws of the United States, in a perfectly legal process. An act of Congress, a simple act of Congress, could save the United States and civilization now if we could find

enough people in the government system to actually bring that about. That's what the whole issue is. You've got to get Obama thrown out of office. If you do not get Obama thrown out of office, it's not that *he* is that important, it's the point that the British Emperor has that aspect. So to get rid of the British, we must get rid of Obama.

Under those conditions, we can effect, because the people in the United States are completely in dismay right now, very little ability to think of doing anything very significant. All it takes is a significant number of people who understand what they're doing, who are going to make the plea to members of Congress and other things, and get the Congress to reform itself and other institutions of the United States to reform themselves, to save the United States! And incidentally, save a lot of other things as well.

Saving Civilization

Question: Lyn, I'm going to read a question from one of people here who wrote it down. His question is: We actually see not just the destruction of people, but the destruction of civilizations themselves. And this should never be allowed, but he asks, what is the relationship to the idea of civilizations that should be saved, and civilization actually developing, to what you talk about when you talk about the character of being human? And what does it mean to be human on this planet?

LaRouche: One of the first things that has to be injected is to get people free of the idea of economy, as people think they understand it. That's where the problem lies. They are not looking at what the principle of action is, which makes progress possible. They're thinking about how something might give them better money, or better this, better that, or better that. But they don't realize how desperate the situation is, in terms of the idea of productivity, in terms of the United States itself.

And what we're doing in most parts of the United States—look, Manhattan has a certain concentration of

If you can inspire people to find that what they're doing is beautiful, and good, and resourceful, that is your best weapon! Only Classical artistic composition can do this. But you must deliver that medication. Here, composer Robert Schumann in a lithograph by Josef Kriehuber, 1839.

effectiveness, but it's a limited case. Most parts of the United States have no competence whatsoever, they've lost it. They don't have the skills. We have people who used to be productive people, they're committing suicide, in various ways. They're destroying themselves.

So you have to create a force, an organized force within the population, which gives some confidence, an expression of confidence, to the people who are out there on the edge of suicide. And I'm talking seriously about the problem of suicide, the problem of mass suicide among the formerly employed people inside the United States is one of the greatest disasters the United States has ever experienced! And this has to be done.

So therefore, I think the question is, how can we utilize the good cause for emergency action to stimulate enough people to recover from this threat, in order to create an army, or a new kind of army which is going to build confidence in the actual people of the United States. If you do that you can win. But we're on the edge! Where the question of whether you can do it or not is still in question.

But for our sake, for the sake of Manhattan, and all similar kinds of things, we must be committed. For example, the music programs we are trying to push along are part of this operation! If you can inspire people, to find that what they're doing is beautiful, and good, and resourceful, that is your best weapon! It's always been the best weapon! Classical artistic composition, and only Classical artistic composition can do this. But Classical artistic composition can do the job! But you must deliver that medication.

Inspire people. You've got to inspire people in the population. And you've got to think about what kinds of people can be inspired! And if you decide you're going to have an army, you're going to organize an army, to make sure that that kind of force is in existence. That's your best chance, probably your only chance.

Every Day Counts
In Today's Showdown
To Save Civilization

That's why you need EIR's **Daily Alert Service**, a strategic overview compiled with the input of Lyndon LaRouche, and delivered to your email 5 days a week.

For example: On Jan. 7, EIR's Daily Alert featured the British hand behind the pattern of global provocations toward war. Of special note is British Intelligence's role in instigating the Saudi Kingdom's attempt to set off a Sunni-Shia war. This religious war has been the intent of British strategy since the Blair-Bush attack on Iraq in 2003.

We also uniquely update you regularly on the progress toward the release of the suppressed 28 pages of the Congressional Inquiry on 9/11, which would expose the Saudi role.

Every edition highlights the reality of the impending financial crash/bail-in policies that would realize the British goal of mass depopulation.

This is intelligence you need to act on, if we are going to survive as a nation and a species. Can you really afford to be without it?

THURSDAY, JANUARY 7, 2016

Volume 2, Number 97

EIR Daily Alert Service

P.O. Box 17390, Washington, DC 20041-0390

- British Crown Pushing War and Genocide in 2016
- Financial Mudslide Goes On; Monetarist Tyranny Gloats over Bail-Ins
- Moody's Downgrades Portugal's Novo Banco
- Puerto Rico's Default: It's Every Vulture for Himself
- Wide Glass-Steagall Debate Set Off Again by Sanders Speech
- MI6 Mouthpiece Evans-Pritchard Touts Persian Gulf Chaos
- North Korea Tests a Miniaturized Hydrogen Bomb
- Uighur Terrorists Found in Indonesia
- Foreign Investors Are Flocking In to China

EDITORIAL

British Crown Pushing War and Genocide in 2016

II. The Future Lies in Eurasia

EIR-Arabic Concludes Successful Week of Action in Egypt

CAIRO, March 20—*EIR*'s southwest Asia specialist and Arabic editor, Hussein Askary, has concluded a very successful one-week trip to Egypt to launch and promote the Arabic translation of *EIR*'s Special Report *The New Silk Road Becomes the World Land-Bridge*, and the ideas within the report. The report and the presentations made by Askary were enthusiastically welcomed by top government officials, economists, and media.

The high point of this intervention was the very high-level and well attended launching of the report under the auspices of the Egyptian Ministry of Transport in a seminar on March 17 at the headquarters of the Ministry, presided over and introduced by Minister Saad El-Geyoushi personally.

Another high point was the reception accorded to Askary on March 20 by the Chairman of the Suez Canal Authority, Admiral Mohab Mamish, the man who oversaw the breathtaking building of the New Suez Canal. Mamish received Askary at his office in Ismailia, located right on the Suez Canal, and attentively listened to a detailed brief-

Hussein Askary

Chairman of the Suez Canal Authority, Admiral Mohab Mamish (left), in his office with Hussein Askary.

ing on the importance of this achievement not only for Egypt's economy, but also for the region and the global economy too, if it is utilized as a development zone and hub for the development corridors stretching from China through southwest Asia to Africa, and also as part of the Maritime Silk Road.

Askary's meeting with Mamish, in which the latter received a gift copy of the report, was preceded by a presentation to the team working under Engineer Nagy Ahmed Amin, Director of the Planning, Research, and Studies Department at the Suez Canal Authority. Askary was later offered a private guided boat tour of the New Suez Canal.

At the launching seminar, Transportation Minister Dr. Saad El-Geyoushi personally presented Askary, as the southwest Asia specialist in *EIR* and representative of the Schiller Institute. In both his introductory remarks and commentary on Askary's presentation, Dr. El-Geyoushi expressed total concordance with the idea of the New Silk Road, and his government's plans to integrate Egypt's transportation networks into the

Transportation Minister Dr. Saad El-Geyoushi

Transportation Minister Dr. Saad El-Geyoushi (left) and Hussein Askary at seminar at the Transportation Ministry.

New Silk Road dynamic. He also took the opportunity to announce that the Egyptian government is intending to invest one trillion Egyptian Pounds ($100 billion) in roads and railways, not only to develop Egypt's transportation network, but also to connect Egypt to Asia and most importantly to Africa to its south, in a 50,000 km network.

The packed hall at the Ministry included top experts and advisors of the ministry and other institutions, and several Egyptian TV and newspapers. Interestingly, the Chinese Arabic TV channel CCTV-Arabic, was present and taped an interview with Askary. Two other TV channels also interviewed Askary.

Sharaf's Evaluation

Two other seminars were organized, one by the Egyptian Society of Engineers (founded in 1920), and another at the Cairo Great Library, which was attended by former Egyptian Prime Minister Dr. Esam Sharaf (also a former Minister of Transport in several Egyptian governments), who was the main commentator on Askary's presentation of the New Silk Road concept. Sharaf expressed his agreement with not only the economic and scientific aspects of the presentation and the report, of which he received a copy, but also with the political, strategic, and cultural aspects too.

Hussein Askary

Hussein Askary (right) presents former Egyptian Prime Minister Esam Sharaf with a copy of the Arabic language version of the Land-Bridge Report. Sharaf had just returned from a long visit to China, and said that the New Silk Road-style projects are "development corridors that can transform all societies" that the projects reach.

He stated that he had just returned from a long visit to China, and that he deeply believed that the New Silk Road is the foundation of "a new and more humane world order, unlike the current order which has degraded human existence and dignity." He also emphasized the point raised in the report, that the New Silk Road and any other such projects "are not mere trade routes, but development corridors that can transform all societies that they reach and the nations that decide to participate in them." He highly recommended that the current Egyptian government take this project seriously and integrate it in its developmental plans and visions. Sharaf expressed his gratitude to *EIR* and the LaRouches personally. He said he has taken note of their ideas and activities for a long time.

In addition to these events, Askary was invited to three TV shows (CBC Extra, Nile Cultural TV, and Nahdha TV) to present the report and the "New World Order" it represents.

The events taking place this week and all the discussions and debates that followed, clearly indicate that the idea of the New Silk Road and World Land-bridge, and the utilization of them for the development of Egypt, the Arab world, and Africa, is regarded as a way to save the Egyptian economy, which has been suffering the terrible consequences of submitting to the trans-Atlantic system and its institutions such as the World Bank and IMF.

Egypt is still suffering economically and socially. In addition, its security situation has been worsened by NATO's unleashing of the jihadist terrorist horces in the region. The urgent demands of the people for reform and betterment of living conditions is pushing President Abdel Fattah El-Sisi and his Prime Minister to resort at times to crisis-management policies.

At the moment of the writing of this report, the Egyptian government is facing a new reshuffling, with eight ministers reportedly being replaced. But the clarity of vision regarding the solutions to this crisis and the resilience and determination shown by the Egyptian people and its leadership represent a great hope for this nation and the region.

Chinese Legislature Pushes Forward China's Leading Role

by William Jones

March 20—The March 5-16 annual session of the National People's Congress (NPC), China's legislature, met at a most crucial moment in world history, as the failed trans-Atlantic system careened towards a near-term all-out economic collapse, while the flag of world leadership has been earned and won by a Eurasia-centered combination, spreading outwards from the China-Russia alliance, to India and the BRICS (Brazil-Russia-India-China-South Africa) nations and the other powers of Eurasia.

In particular, China is the leading nation in today's world, with a leadership most clearly embodied in the fact that China will send the first-ever probe to the far side of the Moon in 2018. It is also embodied in China's revolutionary program of linking up the world with advanced infrastructure development through an extended New Silk Road, which has been the official and very actively practiced policy of China under President Xi Jinping since 2013, under the name of "One Belt, One Road."

But it should also be noted here that the level of China's leading achievements would have been impossible but for its unique alliance with the Russia of master-strategist Vladimir Putin, a China-Russia alliance whose closeness is unprecedented in history, but which also includes India in the "strategic triangle" of the RIC, which was the original seed of the BRICS.

The NPC committed itself to faster advance in science, led by space exploration, and to a deepening of the New Silk Road through "industrial capacity-sharing." As we will describe below, this means rapidly increasing the scientific-technological level of industry in China, while simultaneously using the achievements of Chinese science and technology to plant advanced basic industry in developing countries,— in particular, to bring to China's "One Belt, One Road" partners, the industries needed for their full participation in this multi-faceted historic "Grand Design" project.

In response to the drop in Chinese exports to the deathly ill economies of the United States and Europe, China has chosen to upgrade its industries technologically, while using its machine-tool and allied upper-end capabilities to bring heavy industry to its Eurasian part-

Xinhua Finance 2015-05-12

China's legislature reaffirmed its commitment to linking up the world—One Belt, One Road—with advanced infrastructure in March. Here construction equipment of China Railway Eryuan Engineering Group, a subsidiary of China Railway Group Limited. The subsidiary has won part of the Moscow-Kazan high-speed railroad construction project, in partnership with two Russian companies.

ners. Contrast the thinking behind this, with the mentality which shut down the auto industry and almost all industrial production in the American Midwest, to be replaced by its present industries of heroin addiction and suicide.

The Chinese government also reiterated to the NPC that "the top priority of the financial sector is to support the development of the real economy," as Prime Minister Li Keqiang said. Regulations are being introduced to be sure it does so. One begins to see why the Chinese people are boundlessly optimistic when compared with the slaves of the City of London, Wall Street, and Brussels.

Xinhua

As part of China's shift to knowledge intensive industries, it will continue to expand high-speed rail construction, said Premier Li Keqiang at the NPC, eventually linking 80% of China's cities with high-speed rail. Here four CRH380D high-speed trains, which have a maximum speed of 380 km/hr.

The present terminal collapse of the U.S. and European markets has taken its toll on the Chinese export-industry, which had become, by default, the manufacturing center of the world economy. But rather than emulate the deadheaded leaders of Wall Street, China's leaders have instead hastened their preparations for the next planned upward "leap" in development, aimed at increasing the productive powers of their labor for producing more high-value products, and moving forward with innovation and development to create new industries alongside the down-sized traditional industries. The other part of their plan is "industrial capacity-sharing" to develop heavy industry among China's partners of the "One Belt, One Road." All this will be a formidable task, but the NPC has laid out a blueprint for the way forward. This year's session is particularly important, in that it it is also the year in which the 13th 5-year plan has been introduced.

The key word in the new plan is "innovation." In the Government Work Report presented to NPC delegates on the first day of the session on March 5, Premier Li Keqiang used the word "innovation" 61 times, underlining its importance for the further development of the Chinese economy. The country would move from being a "trader of quantity" into a "trader of quality," Li said, indicating that they would transition from the more labor-intensive to more knowledge-intensive industries. There would also be a push to advance those industries in which China has already gained some international prominence, in particular, in high-speed rail construction. China, Li said, intends to build 8,000 kilometers of rail this year.

"We should also expand major infrastructure projects," Li said, "with the aim of increasing the length of high-speed railways in service to 30,000 kilometers and linking more than 80% of the big cities in China with high-speed railways, building or upgrading around 30,000 kilometers of expressways, and achieving full coverage of access to broadband networks in both urban and rural areas." China will also continue to enhance its role as the primary exporter of high-speed rail, open new economic cooperation corridors and maritime hubs, create an internal logistics network, and intensify cross-border cooperation.

The Silk Road and Shared Development

A new concept unveiled, or rather, newly conceptualized, is the concept of industrial capacity-sharing. This builds on China's current program in building a high-speed transportation grid of connectivity along the Belt and Road. In addition to creating such "connectivity" with its neighbors to the west in central Asia and to the south in Southeast and south Asia, China will also "share" its industrial capacity, in order to create new industrial capacity in the countries along the Belt and Road.

Researcher Zhibo Qiu explained this concept in the Jamestown Foundation's *China Brief* on Sept. 16, 2015, citing Chinese government sources. She wrote, "China is on track to become a net exporter of capital by the end of this year, following a larger shift from exporting low-to-medium-end manufacturing products to exporting high-end manufacturing supply chains and infrastructure development models.

"Rather than relying purely on the export of cheap products, China has moved to export integrated manufacturing supply chains, which span the full range of products, technology, capital, and management, to services and standards. Compared to the pure export of products, industrial capacity cooperation includes infrastructure construction, manufacturing equipment production, technology transfer, professional talents and skilled worker training, as well as operation and maintenance. The industrialization of developing countries will provide cheaper land and labor for Chinese companies to relocate manufacturing bases and establish industrial parks overseas."

The importance of President Xi's initiative of the "Belt and Road," the Silk Road Economic Belt, and the 21st Century Maritime Silk Road, was further underlined as a major foreign policy objective at Foreign Minister Wang Yi's press conference on March 7. "Today over 70 nations and international organizations have expressed interest and over 30 countries have signed agreements with us to build the Belt and Road," Wang Yi said. "The Belt and Road Initiative is China's idea, but its opportunities belong to the world. This initiative echoes the general call of Asian and European countries for development and cooperation. It shows that China is transitioning rapidly from a participant in the international system to a provider of public goods. In building the Belt and Road, we follow the principle of wide consultation, joint con-

Xinhua/Agung Pambudhy

China's Foreign Minister Wang Yi said over 30 countries have signed agreements with China to build the Belt and Road. Although it "is China's idea," he said, "its opportunities belong to the world." Here a signing ceremony for an Indonesia-China joint venture for high-speed rail from Jakarta to Bandung. From left to right: Director General of Railways of Indonesia's Transportation Ministry, Herman Dwiatmoki, Indonesian Minister of Transportation Ignasius Jonan, and Hanggoro Budi Wiryawan, president director of KCIC, the joint venture.

tribution and shared benefit. It is an open initiative, not ... expansionism. What it unfolds before the world will be a new historical painting of shared development and prosperity on the entire Eurasian continent." Wang Yi noted that work is already proceeding on the Budapest-Belgrade Railway and the Jakarta-Bandung High-speed Railway. And important steps have been taken in the China-Laos Railway and China-Thailand Railway, both parts of the Pan-Asia Railway Network.

Finance Must Serve Real Economy

With the expansion of the economy and the lack of a comprehensive commercial banking system, much of the funding of small- and medium-sized enterprises (SMEs) in China has been forced into the realm of "shadow banking," including the burgeoning Internet banking, which has lacked all forms of regulation. This is particularly important for China today in that much of the "innovation" needed in the Chinese economy will come from the SMEs. China has long viewed the German industry's *Mittelstand* as a model for this type of innovation economy, but has lacked the means for financing it. The large state-owned banks which have

The crucial role of science and technology was heavily emphasized at the NPC. The government will increase the budget for R&D. Here the C919, China's first domestically produced large passenger aircraft at a plant near Shanghai.

dominated in the Chinese financial system have preferred lending to the larger industries, feeling that their investments there were more secure.

Now China is intent on creating a functioning system of commercial banks which are subject to strict financial regulation. Banking Regulatory Commission head Shang Fulin outlined the principles required for the functioning of such banks.

• First, the loans must be beneficial to the development of the real economy.

• Secondly, they must be aimed at lowering financial risks.

• And thirdly, the loans must be beneficial to the rights of the investor as well as the creditor.

"The banks have to know the real target of their investments," Shang said. Shang also underlined the need for creating a bank "firewall."

Problems in China's financial system have been grossly exaggerated in the lying trans-Atlantic press. Indeed, foreign intervention from London by such as George Soros, and speculation on housing shortages in major cities have led to problems, although it must be underlined that these have no resemblance to those in the trans-Atlantic financial system which is blowing out. There is housing speculation, but there are no housing-backed derivatives, for example, like those which blew out the Wall Street system in 2007-2008.

To address the problems which do exist, a number of regulatory plans, some wise and others questionable, were under discussion during the NPC.

China's underlying principle of financial reform was emphasized by Premier Li at the concluding press conference on March 16. "The top priority of the financial sector is to support the development of the real economy," Li told reporters. We are in the process of developing a "full-fledged financial regulatory regime," he said. "The financial system often operates according to its own laws," Li warned. "Therefore, we should watch out for possible risks. We have to guard against risk and moral hazard."

The Crucial Role of Science

The crucial element in creating an innovative economy is the rapid development of science and technology. China will increase the government budget devoted to R&D to 2.5%. Accelerating the development of scientific research will be crucial in this plan. "We should launch new national science and technology programs," Li said in his Work Report, "build first-class national science centers and technological innovation hubs, help develop internationally competitive high-innovation enterprises, and establish pilot reform zones for all-round innovation." In his Government Work Report, he underlined three major achievements of Chinese science in 2015:

• The development of a new jet airliner,

• The development of a new high-resolution imaging satellite, and

• The advances made in space exploration.

The crucial role of space science was emphasized by the many representatives of the space program who were delegates to the NPC, including China's first woman astronaut, Liu Yang. Speaking to the press on March 6, Wu Ji, the director of China's Space Science Center, said: "If you want to innovate, you must have knowledge of the sciences. Space science is inseparable from China's innovation-driven development."

According to Wu Ji, a 15-year space science strategy has been mapped out by the Center, which will tackle questions such as the formation and evolution of the universe, extra-terrestrial intelligence, extra-solar planets, and other questions.

"If China wants to be a strong global nation," he said, "it should not only care about immediate interests, but also contribute to humankind. Only that can win China the real respect of the world."

What Wu Ji didn't mention, but what is absolutely revolutionary, is the planned landing of the first-ever probe on the far side of the Moon in 2018. This will be a major breakthrough for all mankind.

Xinhua/Li Xiang

China's Space Center has mapped out a 15-year space science strategy, as a contribution to humankind. Here a model of the Shenzhou-10 manned spacecraft docked with the Tiangong-1 space module, during a 2013 exhibit for the public.

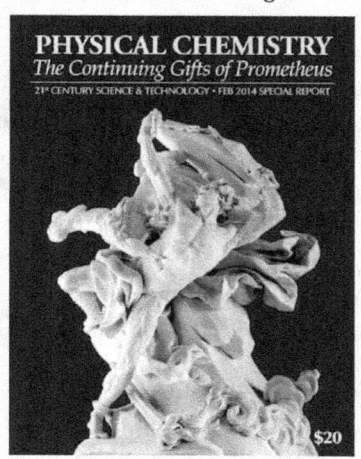
While the issues of fundamental space science are absolutely critical for deepening our understanding of our own Earth, our Galaxy, and the galaxies around it, the element which most captures the popular imagination is manned space exploration. Liu Yang, China's first woman astronaut (photo page four) and a delegate from the People's Liberation Army to the Congress, therefore attracted a great deal of attention from reporters and delegates and gave a number of widely circulated interviews.

Speaking to reporters, Liu Yang said that the launch this year of the Tiangong-2 space lab and the Shenzhou-11 manned spacecraft will be very important. It will put two astronauts in space for 30 days rather than the 16 days in previous missions. "It's a big breakthrough and a great leap forward," Liu said. "The increase from 16 days to 30 days is not just numbers, but a great improvement in technical support, such as environmental control and life-support technology. We need to create an environment in space that is similar to that on Earth. That's a big technological breakthrough."

Ye Peijian, Chief Designer of China's Lunar Exploration Program, hopes that China will be able to carry out a successful mission to Mars by 2021, the 100th anniversary of the founding of the Communist Party of China.

India's New Self-Conception As a World Power

by Helga Zepp-LaRouche, founder of the Schiller Institutes

March 16—India is no longer just the Subcontinent, but clearly is changing its own identity so as to become one of the future major players in the world, since it will soon bypass the population size of China, and already has the highest economic growth rate internationally.

That self-confidence, which clearly has been boosted since Narendra Modi became Prime Minister almost two years ago, was very visible at the inaugural meeting of the Raisina Dialogue, the new flagship conference of the Indian government, which was hosted by India's Ministry of Foreign Affairs in association with the Observer Research Foundation, from March 1 to 3 in New Delhi. Over 100 speakers from 40 countries, including several serving foreign ministers and former presidents from Asia, before an audience of 600 institutional representatives, focussed for three days on issues of stronger Asian integration, as well as better integration of Asia with the rest of the world.

India is extremely important, both as one of the cradles of human civilization with an over 5,000-year old continuous history and culture, as well as for the rich contributions India can make to a future peaceful world order based on its great historical periods and great minds of the past, such as the Vedic writings, the Gupta period of classical literature, the Indian Renaissance, Rabindranath Tagore, or Mahatma Gandhi, to only touch on highlights. With a very young population, 65% under the age of 35, and an urban middle-class that has grown to about 430 million, with an ambitious hi-tech orientation and a visionary space program, India is set to become a science driver economy for the whole world.

Therefore, one big question will be whether the present Indian leadership will find a way to put primary

EIRNS/Kasia Kruczkowski

Helga Zepp-LaRouche spoke March 2, 2016 in New Delhi at the inaugural meeting of the Indian government-sponsored Raisina Dialogue to foster stronger Asian integration. She is shown here second from the left among other speakers.

emphasis on a new paradigm with the BRICS countries—which Modi has called the first alliance of countries whose importance is not defined by their present capacities, but by their future potential,— or whether the country will be bogged down in a narrower geopolitical view, which makes it susceptible to various hot-button issues, such as those of Pakistan, border conflicts, and religious tensions.

At the Raisina Dialogue both directions were present, conforming

PIB

Indian Prime Minister Narendra Modi has called the organization the first alliance of countries whose importance is determined by their future potential. Here, Modi (center) handing over homes at a project site in the nation of Sri Lanka last March.

to the present view of the Indian Establishment that there should be openness to all sides, as a balance between those who want India to be primarily part of the BRICS, and those who would rather work with the Anglo-American powers as a geopolitical counter to Russia and China.

Differing Voices

India's Foreign Minister Sushma Swaraj emphasized the importance of connectivity, not only for India and the entire south Asian region, but also for all of the Asian continent, in her keynote address at the opening of the conference. She promised that India would win over "vested interests" to this perspective.

Earlier, the first speaker, Ms. Chandrika Bandaranaike Kumaratunga, former President of Sri Lanka, was emphatic in stressing the need to build trust and confidence among the countries of the region, and the need to establish a new paradigm in the policies of the governments whereby the new generations that were born after the Partition leave conflict behind, and look forward to the future development of the region.

She stressed that the conflict between India and Pakistan had hindered the development of the region badly, holding regional cooperation hostage for 70 years. She underlined the importance of India and China joining hands for regional development, which is now possible through China's "One Belt, One Road" policy. China's

economic power should be seen as an opportunity, rather as a threat. Ms. Kumaratunga said that Sri Lanka could be a bridge for all south Asian nations, since it has good relations with all of them.

The former President of Afghanistan, Hamid Karzai, argued exactly in the same direction. He called India Afghanistan's best friend, but also said that his country's relationship with China is comprehensive, and that Kabul has an important role to play as a transit hub for regional economic integration. "Afghanistan wants the best possible relations between India and China,—there is a need for positive symmetry," Karzai stressed, and expressed hope that the China-Iran rail line would be extended to other countries.

Afghanistan wants to be a bridge between south Asia, central Asia, India, and China, he continued. "Afghanistan represents the shortest route between China and Iran, India and central Asia, and Russia and central Asia. Afghanistan fully supports India's policy on central Asia and China's "One Belt One Road" policy. Karzai praised the revival of the ancient silk road by China as the way to make all of south Asia prosperous.

But also relations with India's neighbors in the East and North are undergoing important transformations. Bangladeshi Foreign Minister Abul Hassan Mahmood Ali, said that the newly formed Bangladesh-Bhutan-India-Nepal (BBIN) sub-regional cooperative architecture will be a game-changer for the entire south Asian region. He said that Bangladesh's vision was to become a middle-income country by 2021. "Water resources management and the blue economy provide tremendous opportunity for the growth of regional economy," and it is connectivity that will help the south Asian nations realize their dreams of prosperity.

The keynote speech by Seychelles founding President Sir James Mancham was also very well received. He emphasized that for the Republic of Seychelles, whose 110 islands cover a maritime space as large as the Federal Republic of Germany with a population of less than 100,000 people, the emphasis the Indian Government gives to the Indian Ocean is obviously of the greatest importance.

He recalled the importance of the Nonaligned Movement during the 1960s, when he first became involved in politics, and throughout the Cold War period. During that period, India's foreign policy was based on the peaceful teachings of such men of wisdom as Rabindranath Tagore, Mahatma Gandhi, and Buddha.

He recalled that India, in its capacity as a leader of the Nonaligned Movement, opposed the effort by the United States to build up a U.S. naval base in Diego Garcia to replace the British, after the British had decided to pull out of "East of Suez." This was a timely reminder in light of the recent British announcement that they intended to renew their East of Suez ambitions.

At that earlier time, Sir James Mancham underlined, India and the Soviet Union had proclaimed the Indian Ocean a zone of peace, and condemned the arrival of the United States in Diego Garcia. He expressed his regret that today India is aligned with the United States to counterbalance the Chinese presence in the area. He also articulated his shock that, at a recent Berlin conference, a high NATO official admitted that the world defense budget is three or four times

Press Information Bureau of India

Adm. Harry B. Harris, Commander, United States Pacific Command, introduced the opposing view, asserting that India will be the defining partner for America's pivot to Asia. He emphasized joint future military maneuvers involving India, Japan, Australia, and the United States. Here Indian and foreign naval ships in an exercise in the Bay of Bengal on Feb. 9, 2016.

higher than what the world is spending on human resources development.

Military strength is too often accompanied by the conviction that "Might makes right." The ugly sight of the destroyed cities in Syria should make us mindful of the power of destruction, even without the use of nuclear weapons.

Notably, an opposing view was brought into the conference by another keynote speaker, Navy Adm. Harry B. Harris, the commander of the U.S. Pacific Command, who asserted that India will be the defining partner for America's rebalance to Asia, and that this will even be the "defining partnership for America in the Twenty-first Century." "Let's be ambitious together," Harris demanded, especially emphasizing past and future joint military maneuvers between India, Japan, Australia, and the United States. It was somewhat unclear who he meant,— or if he meant it ironically,— when he said that some countries "seek to bully" smaller nations through intimidation and coercion, and which countries he referred to as "building castles on sand."

Indian Concerns

The most delicate concern for India for historical, political, and military reasons is obviously the relation with Pakistan, and it was only three months ago that Prime Minister Modi paid a surprise visit to this country on his birthday, in an obvious effort to improve the situation. Equally obvious also was the effort by some panelists at the conference to put salt into Indian wounds by blasting Pakistan as a country that should be charged with state terrorism.

"Let's punish Pakistan together," an American speaker agitated, rubbing an obvious raw nerve of many in the audience. Given the fact that both countries have nuclear arsenals, one can only wonder about the motives behind such suggestions. The discussion of terrorism was solely focussed on Pakistan, leaving out completely the role of Saudi financing of various terrorist organizations and the concerns which former DIA head General Michael Flynn has expressed repeatedly about geopolitical considerations of the United States itself in this matter.

Under present circumstances there is both concern among some in India about the China-Pakistan economic corridor linking China's Xinjiang Province to Pakistan's Gwadar Port, and about the decision of the Obama Administration to sell eight F-16 fighter planes to Pakistan, an action for which U.S. Ambassador Richard Verma was summoned to the Ministry of External Affairs to listen for 45 minutes to the expression of "displeasure" by Foreign Secretary Subrahmanyam Jaishankar.

In its totality, the Raisina Dialogue conference brought together a vibrant multitude of subjects and speakers, expressing an overall tendency of integrating India and south Asia more deeply with Asia at large and with the world. Whether for diplomatic or other reasons, what was completely absent however, was any discussion about the horrendous condition of the trans-Atlantic financial system, and how the Asian nations can protect themselves against the consequences of the pending blowout.

The potential to resolve all remaining geopolitical issues and potential flare-up points on a higher level of reason assuredly exists. What do you do, when one seems to have a seemingly insurmountable conflict with another person or state? It is important to find the higher level of reason, so that the antagonisms of the existing paradigm can be superseded. How can the unresolved tensions between China and India, often manipulated by outside forces based on maps and conflicts stemming from a geopolitical past, be overcome? If Russia, China, and India work together, as it has been concretely proposed already, to pacify and economically develop southwest Asia, that higher level of common interest can be established.

The concrete potential for such an intervention has been created through President Putin's brilliant defusing of the Syrian war, first by the Russian military intervention starting September of last year, which created the preconditions for a political solution, and just now, the sudden troop withdrawal of Russian forces, after the mission was successfully accomplished. As the Chinese representative, Vice Foreign Minister Li Baodong, had emphasized at the Vienna Syria peace conference, the rebuilding of Syria must start immediately, so that the population can see the peace dividend of hope and of life becoming normal again.

In his recent journey to Saudi Arabia, Egypt, and Iran, Chinese President Xi Jinping explicitly offered to extend the New Silk Road, "One Belt, One Road" policy to southwest Asia. Shortly thereafter, the first Silk Road train arrived in Tehran from Yiwu, thus creating the potential to extend that line to Baghdad, Damascus, and all the way to Cairo. Both China, offering a "win-win" approach for all nations participating in this policy, and India, with its very good relations with all the countries of southwest Asia, can add the necessary economic dimension to the peace perspective which Russia has now made possible.

This moment represents a precious opportunity to use the rebuilding of the war-torn nation of Syria as a game-changer to bring the perspective of a real economic development plan onto the table for the whole region from Afghanistan to the Mediterranean, from the Caucasus to the Persian Gulf. If the strong neighbors work together it is possible—because then, and only then, will their client states be brought under control. The collaboration of foreign ministers Kerry and Lavrov has opened the way, and European nations such as Germany, Italy, France, and others can be brought on board, since this is the only way that the refugee crisis can be solved.

India, as the up-and-coming world power—based on a beautiful philosophical tradition which maintains that the cosmic order must inform life and conduct on earth, and based on the inspiration of its founder Mahatma Gandhi for a peaceful world—can shape the future with a new paradigm for all of mankind.

Balkan Countries Look To Join China's New Silk Road

March 14—The following is an interview done by Feride Istogu-Gillesberg with Iljaz Spahiu, the head of the Albanian-Chinese Cultural Institute in Tirana, for the German paper Neue Solidarität.

Spahiu has occupied himself with Chinese language, culture, society, and politics for 40 years. He earned a degree in Chinese language and literature at Beijing University during 1974-1978. Among other assignments, Spahiu worked for more than two decades as a translator and journalist for Radio Tirana. From 2002 to 2006 he served as a diplomat in the Albanian embassy in Beijing, and then worked for a private company there for several years. At the same time he was the Chinese correspondent for Radio Free Asia in Washington. He has also translated two novels by Chinese author Mo Yan.

Feride Istogu-Gillesberg: China and Albania have had a long standing relationship. How do you see relations between China and Albania today?

Iljaz Spahiu: As you yourself said, Albania and China have had a traditional historical relationship, which began in the 1960s and lasted until the end of the 1970s. This developed into a special relationship: China defined it as "friends and brothers," and the Albanians described it as "strong as granite and pure as crystal." You also have to recognize that, independent of this relationship's ideological foundation, a real friendship emerged between the two peoples which is still very much alive today.

Back then (in the 1960s and 70s) Albanian films had a huge influence on the education of an entire generation in China. According to the statistics, the 1967 movie *Victory over Death* has had the greatest viewership in the entire world.[1] Unfortunately, at the end of the 1970s, when China began to open up to the world, Albania pursued a path of total isolation.

al.chine-embassy.org

Iljaz Spahiu (left) with China's Ambassador to Albania, Jiang Yu.

After a fifteen-year hiatus, at the beginning of the 1990s relations between our two countries began to normalize. The basis for the relationship is different now; it is a relationship of mutual advantage, but the old traditional relationship provides strong support for further deepening it on both sides. At the moment there exists a good relationship and a stable policy on the basis of mutual advantage, free of ideology. Three joint declarations have been signed between the two nations, and there have been important, high-level visits.

The degree of economic cooperation certainly doesn't match the political; although over the past year we have had a noticeable uptick in trade, yet there is hardly any Chinese investment in Albania to speak of. I recommend using the traditional friendship, the special image of Albania, the fondness and nostalgia for Albania which the currently ruling generation in China has, and further developing and strengthening the relationship this way.

You have to keep in mind that China today is a per-

---

1. The film ("Ngadhnjim mbi vdekjen" in Albanian), about the World War II heroine Bule Naipi, had more than 100 million viewers in China.

manent member of the UN Security Council, it is the second largest economy in the world, and an actor on the international political stage of growing significance.

Eurasian Land-Bridge

Istogu-Gillesberg: Helga Zepp-LaRouche, the founder of the Schiller Institutes, is the author of the report *The New Silk Road Becomes the World Land-Bridge*.[2] Mrs. Zepp-LaRouche has spoken at many international conferences about the great significance of the development of the Silk Road—not only for China and the BRICS nations, but for the entire world. Collaboration around economic development is the hope of mankind. The development of infrastructure, agriculture, and industrial production is the basis for raising living standards for all humanity, and the means for securing peace—as is now more or less coming to Syria. Does China have an agreement with Albania for the extension of the Silk Road, the strategy of "One Belt, One Road?"

Spahiu: First of all, I happily can say that the "One Belt, One Road" initiative, as well as the program for cooperation among the "16+1,"[3] is creating an extraordinary opportunity—not only for the development of Albania, but for the entire Balkan peninsula.

China has plenty of capital, as well as extensive technical and human capabilities. It has the will and the desire to expand alliances for trade into Europe. On the other hand, our countries need investment in the construction of infrastructure and the development of our economies.

In the framework of the "One Belt, One Road" initiative, Albania is pursuing significant projects which are now negotiated and are only awaiting concretization. The most significant of these projects are the highway from Arbrit,[4] the "Blue Corridor,"[5] energy proj-

Xinhua/Gao Jie

Iljaz Spahiu emphasized that China's "One Belt, One Road" initiative and its cooperation with Central and Eastern Europe is creating an extraordinary opportunity for Albania and the rest of the Balkan peninsula.

ects, and the construction of industrial parks, agriculture, and tourism—among other things.

The Albanian government is staying in constant contact with its Chinese partner around the realization of these projects. The Albanian Prime Minister has met the Chinese Prime Minister three times at high-level summit meetings, in the context of the 16+1. Currently, several chairmen of Chinese enterprises are stationed in Tirana, only awaiting the realization of these projects. In the meantime, other companies are showing interest in investing in Albania, because they see Albania as part of trade in the Balkans and beyond.

It must be stressed that, because of its traditional friendship with China, Albania has an advantage. Fortunately, this friendship is not only nurtured in the population, but also in our governments and leadership circles.

Certainly there are obstacles, especially of a technical sort—mainly in the area of financing, because Albania has huge foreign debts—but these can be overcome through a common determination.

Istogu-Gillesberg: How do you see the role of the Balkans in connection with the strategy of "One Belt, One Road?"

Spahiu: The "One Belt, One Road" initiative has given new content and a new dynamic to the program of cooperation of the "16+1" and the Balkan countries. These are countries through which the Silk Road travels. They will profit from this initiative; it opens up for us an excellent perspective for development. This ini-

---

2. https://worldlandbridge.com/
3. China's cooperation with 16 countries of Southeastern and Central Europe.
4. The connection by highway between Tirana, Albania, and Skopje (Former Yugoslav Republic of Macedonia).
5. The Adriatic-Ionian highway, which connects Greece with Slovenia along the Adriatic coast.

tiative provides the Balkan countries with the possibility of trade links and cooperation with China as a trading partner.

In addition, the Balkan region serves as a bridge, or connecting point, between China and Europe. Thanks to these ongoing initiatives ("One Belt, One Road"), important projects are currently being carried out in the Balkan peninsula, especially in infrastructure and the energy sector, financed by China. These projects will have an important influence on the development of the whole Balkan region. Noteworthy in this connection is the project for extension of the rail connection between Piraeus-Skopje-Belgrade-Budapest, which shortens the route between China and Europe and expands trade, as well as the construction of highways in Serbia, the Former Yugoslav Republic of Macedonia, and Montenegro, which will make cooperation between the Balkan countries easier and more profitable.

Role of Confucianism

Istogu-Gillesberg: Helga Zepp-LaRouche has often emphasized the importance of cultural cooperation among nations. You have at your command great knowledge about the history and philosophy of China. What can we learn from the Chinese philosopher Confucius?

Spahiu: That's right. Cultural collaboration has an irreplaceable significance for strengthening and further developing relations among nations. Through cultural exchange and personal contact you can facilitate mutual knowledge of the culture, history, mentality, and values on both sides, which make it possible to bring people closer together. The Albanian-Chinese Cultural Institute has as its chief mission the nurturing and strengthening of the relationship between our two countries: Our chief concern is to transmit this relationship to the young generation in both countries.

The Institute is playing an important role as a bridge between the two cultures, establishing close ties between the generations, the media, and philosophical thought, and providing the basis for getting to know one another and the exchange of values.

As to Confucius's philosophy, I think that it is a precious possession of not only the Chinese, but for people worldwide. Confucian culture has gone through many ups and downs; it was undervalued and ignored for thousands of years, but in the end, its values have gained a new degree of importance, especially over the recent years, when the western economies are shrinking and those of the Asian nations, especially China, are growing. The values which have been preached by Confucian culture—such as commitment, a sense of responsibility, the spirit of sacrifice, community, and advanced education, among other things—have undoubtedly created the circumstances for favorable economic and social development in Asia.

In this context, you can say that the onrushing development of Asia is competing with the modernity of the West. You can furthermore pose the question of whether the economic development of the Confucian societies of Asia opens up a new path to a modernization with Confucian characteristics, which differs from that in the West. The value system which dominates Chinese society ultimately has its roots in Confucius' philosophy, which was not only dominant in the golden ages of Chinese history, but also shapes China's societal values in large measure today.

In this respect the system of values with Chinese characteristics has been further elaborated, established, and recognized step by step. These values base themselves on the harmonization of the values of the individual with the progress of society as a whole, in contrast to the value system of the West, where individual freedom is emphasized.

In order to analyze the significance of Confucian culture and its ideas and concepts for today's society, there was an international symposium on the theme "Confucianism—Peaceful Development on Earth," held in September of last year in Beijing on the occasion of Confucius' 2,565th birthday. One idea which was presented at this symposium was that traditional Chinese cultural thought, and its humanistic spirit, civilized ideas, and moral concepts, can play a positive role in the world's getting to know and transforming itself, as well as in the administration and improvement of governance.

Istogu-Gillesberg: Do you have any closing words for our German readers?

Spahiu: I want to thank you for giving me the opportunity for this interview, to be able to communicate with German readers, for whom I have always had great respect.

Since this interview deals with the subject of China, I would recommend that you make yourselves familiar with Chinese culture and history. Only in this way can you achieve an objective view of China's political situation, economic development, and communication in the world.

Linking Afghanistan to the World

by Tanu Maitra

March 20—Afghanistan borders south Asia, the Middle East, and central Asia, and yet it is one of the most isolated countries in the world. Decades of foreign invasion, destruction, and internal chaos have intensified its isolation. It has, for example no national rail system. Indeed, it has almost no railroads at all.

The International North-South Transport Corridor (INSTC) will link Afghanistan to the world—to south Asia, southeast Asia, east Asia and China by land and sea. The INSTC multimodal transportation system runs from India, through Iran, to Russia and northern Europe (*EIR*, March 18). Its eastern leg will run from the Iranian city of Chabahar on the Gulf of Oman, through Zahedan (in Iran, where Iran meets Pakistan and Afghanistan), to Herat (Afghanistan), a route of more than 1,400 kilometers.

"India has shown a willingness to establish a railway route linking Chabahar and Herat, and this is a milestone toward connecting Afghanistan to Chabahar port," reported Afghanistan's *Tolo News*, quoting Mahdi Rohani, a spokesman for Iran's Ministry of Public Works on March 13. At present, Afghanistan has only two short rail links—a 75 km link in the north between Mazar-e-Sharif and Hairatan on the Uzbekistan border, and a just-built short link that connects Herat in Afghanistan with Khaf, Iran, a length of 140 km.

The development of Chabahar port in Iran and the rail line to Herat, Afghanistan, is immediately on the agenda. India's proposed plan to develop the port is seemingly ready after months of delay. The agreement for the first phase will be signed at the Maritime

India Summit 2016, April 14-16, in Mumbai. Iran's Port and Maritime Authority has awarded a ten-year port development project to Iranian firm Arya Bandar, which will in turn sign an agreement with Indian Ports Global Pvt Ltd, the Indian news daily *The Hindu* reported on March 15.

The plan for the port will make it more than a node point for the INSTC. It will contribute to developing

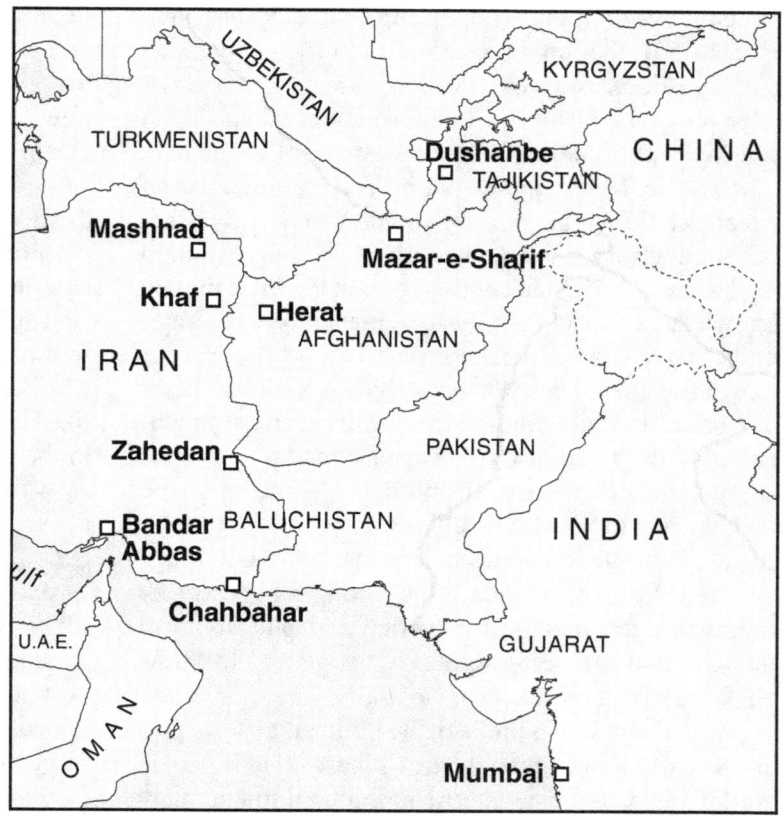

The eastern leg of the International North-South Transport Corridor will include a container terminal at Chabahar, Iran, on the Gulf of Oman and a rail line from Chabahar through Zahedan to Herat, Afghanistan. Iran and India are also ready to sign an agreement for an undersea natural gas pipeline from Chabahar to the coast of Gujarat State in India. The gas will come from Turkmenistan.

U.S. Embassy, Kabul/S.K. Vemmer

Herat, Afghanistan, in 2011. Its population was 10,795 in 2006, at the time of the last census.

Chabahar as a manufacturing and trading center. At the last census in 2006, Chabahar's population was 71,000. Reports indicate that India is ready to invest $31 billion in this project over a period of years. The first phase, expected to be launched next month, will include construction and operation of two berths, a container terminal of 640 meters' length and a multi-purpose cargo terminal of 600 meters.

The second phase will include building the railroad to Herat and development of a special economic zone as part of the Chabahar port complex. The zone is planned by a number of India's private and public sector investors, such as the Jindal Infrastructures, the petroleum refiner Essar, and the Indian state-run steel manufacturer SAIL. Iran has agreed to allocate to India the required land for the zone.

Undersea Gas Pipeline to India

There is also a plan for an undersea gas pipeline from Chabahar port to India. India's *Tribune News* reported March 17, citing an unnamed "top official" of India's Modi government, that India is set to sign a deal with Iran for a direct undersea gas pipeline from Chabahar port to the coast of Gujarat state in India. The $4.5 billion, 1,400 km undersea gas pipeline will bring 31.5 million standard cubic meters of gas per day from Iran to India's west coast. The gas, which originates in gas-rich Turkmenistan, will be piped across Iran to Chabahar port.

Iran is in a hurry to develop the INSTC eastern leg and is pushing India to speed up its investments The project is of great economic importance to India as well, since New Delhi is keen to broaden its economic relations with Iran and expand its trade into central Asia.

The Afghan View, and China

Afghanistan's Chief Executive Abdullah Abdullah traveled to Chabahar port last January, during his three-day visit to Iran, and surveyed the project's capabilities and capacities. The presence of a cargo terminal in Chabahar port will provide Afghanistan with a new outlet to the sea in addition to the port of Gwadar, Pakistan, and promises a significant boost to its role in regional and global markets. Expressing the importance of the project, Abdullah Abdullah also made a commitment that, when developed, Afghanistan will use the port to trade with the Asian countries. Afghanistan's high cost of trade via Pakistan is a concern. The customs tariffs levied on good imported into Afghanistan through Pakistan are also high.

Iran has also sought to interest China in the project. China faces a problem with pirates in the Mediterranean and the Gulf of Aden, which appears to have a significant influence on its foreign trade. The development of Chabahar port and its linkage to the INSTC will improve China's access to parts of central Asia, particularly west of the Caspian Sea, and to Afghanistan. At present, Chinese goods are shipped to the Iranian port of Bandar Abbas and Chabahar through the port of Dubai, about 800 km further west More direct access to INSTC through Chabahar port would help China.

Iran has already invited Chinese investments in its southeastern province of Sistan-Balochistan and has urged Chinese enterprises to participate in a series of projects in Chabahar, including the development of a rail network as well as key petrochemical and steel projects.

LaRouche South Africa for BRICS, Nuclear Power, Faces Off Against British Regime Change

As South Africa and Brazil continue to face waves of regime change assault from the British Empire, La-Rouche South Africa has been providing a standard of truth on the strategic issues—the issues of the BRICS and nuclear power as the engines of national sovereignty, progress, and prosperity, and has been naming the names of the opposing, British-steered regime changers. Ramasimong Phillip Tsokolibane, leader of LaRouche South Africa, has recently released the following "fighting words."

A DECISION THAT CANNOT BE DELAYED
Time to Kick the British Empire To the Curb

March 14—As the spokesman for the movement of American statesman and economist Lyndon LaRouche in South Africa, I warmly applaud the opening of the New Development Bank of the BRICS and the current hiring of staff for its African branch in Johannesburg.

This new bank, headquartered in Shanghai, is the centerpiece of a new global economic order emerging from Eurasia, one that can replace the decadent and totally bankrupt, monetarist trans-Atlantic financial system, dominated by the British Empire and its Wall Street satrapy. The leadership of the new bank has already stated its intention to provide precisely the credit for development that the City of London and Wall Street have withheld. And it is credit for development that is the most potent weapon against the drive for war and chaos now unleashed by the dying British Empire and its financial system.

For South Africa, and for Africa as a whole, the development initiatives of fellow BRICS members Russia, China, and India—as President Zuma stated recently, including in his State of the Nation remarks—are precisely the means to combat unemployment and raise the productive capacities of all of our peoples, enabling an emergence from the shackles of imperialist policy that has treated us not as human beings with a God-given capacity to create, but as mere beasts, whose

Citizens Electoral Council, Australia
Ramasimong Phillip Tsokolibane leads LaRouche South Africa.

cost of maintenance can no longer be sustained, and whose burdensome costs must be eliminated through mass slaughter by any means necessary. This is the long-stated policy of global genocide of His Royal Virus Prince Philip, the cadaver-like consort of the bitch Queen of the British Empire.

We never asked to be part of the British Empire. It was originally imposed on us by force of arms. Our people have never been treated as anything more than useful beasts by these imperial masters. And now finally, as our government takes us into alliance with the peaceful but powerful forces of Eurasia that comprise the heart of the BRICS alliance, we have started, finally, to walk down the road once envisioned by the great Mandela. It is a pathway that will lead to the long overdue development of the nations and peoples of Africa, emerging from the darkness of imperial rule and enforced backwardness. It is a pathway that will see our nation, with its proud cadre of scientists and engineers, playing an important role in placing mankind as a whole back on the road to become true masters of our solar system, of our galaxy, and of the universe beyond.

And yet, and yet ... Even with great vistas opening unto us, we remain inside that Empire of our oppressors, which calls itself the British Commonwealth. Why is that?

Let me be clear: There are two pathways before us. The policy of the British Empire and its degenerate Royal Family and their financial retainers in the global banking system, is to kill six billion or more people globally. The BRICS are the enemy of this policy. The differences are irreconcilable. Listen to the rantings of that servant of the British Empire, the American President Barack Obama, against Russia and China, and see clearly that a potential thermonuclear war looms on the near horizon. Despite the efforts of good men and women to seek peace—and efforts of Russian President Vladimir Putin, especially, to secure such peace, including in Syria and elsewhere—as long as Obama remains with his shaky fingers on the nuclear trigger, the war danger remains.

We cannot walk down these two divergent paths. We must, in the name of our progeny and of all mankind, make our choice now and for the future. I say, stand and fight for a new just world economic order, the one that Mandela sought, and the one that Putin's Russia and the Chinese propose to bring into existence. I say put both feet on that path, and with the sense of urgency that these times demand, let us remove ourselves from all institutions of the British Empire. I say, as I have before, toss all the pictures of the Queen and her family into the bonfire of history. It is high time that we finally grow into the beckoning greatness that we must be, as the leader of a new and developing Africa.

IT'S GAME ON!

To Stop Regime Change, Dump the British Empire!

March 11—The riotous events engulfing our campuses fit nicely into the pattern that we have exposed in articles published in 2014 and 2015—a pattern of events intended to promote so-called 'regime change', orchestrated by forces linked to the British Empire and its stooge and murderous thug, the American President Barack Obama. The target is not the Zuma government, although the character of the demands made by the students, and the London assets that support them, might lead one to think that. The target is the nation of South Africa, and South Africa's intent to play a globally important leadership role in rescuing the world from the dying imperial trans-Atlantic system. We are on a course to do that through our involvement in the BRICS alliance and related global development programs, such as China's New Silk Road by land and sea, as well as our support for the efforts of Russian President Putin to secure peace in the face of the British-orchestrated terrorism in Syria and elsewhere.

Thus, the demonstrators are pawns in a game whose ultimate objective is not a mere change in the Presidency of South Africa, but national chaos, in support of the intention of the Bitch Queen of the British Empire and her retinue, to slaughter some six billion or more of the world's people alive today, including most, if not all, Africans.

I applaud the recent, public acknowledgment by African National Congress Secretary General Gwede Mantashe that the U.S. government is working for 'regime change' in South Africa. Such statements alone, however, will not stop those organising the regime change, including many London toadies and stooges in this country, including such loudmouths as Julius Malema, sometimes known as the English Sausage. The puppet-masters, including operatives sanctioned by Obama and Washington—and linked to such institutions as Wits University, the University of Johannesburg, *Business Day*, and the *Mail & Guardian*—will not be deterred by words or exposure alone. What is required is a clear statement, such as I have delivered above, of what is behind this drive. The background is contained in articles published by the LaRouche movement and its EIR News Service, links to which are appended for the edification of patriots, and as a political laxative that might allow us to release the kak that clogs our political system.

Also required is a statement of intent to break, once and for all, with the genocidal policies of the British Empire and its Royal Family of mass murderers. We must break the political, and most importantly, the intellectual shackles of our colonial bondage to London, and exit all the institutions of the Empire. We must have the courage to walk away from the dying trans-Atlantic system and fully embrace the new, just world economic order, for which the New Development Bank (NDB) of the BRICS—whose African branch will be proudly headquartered in Johannesburg—is the seed crystal.

We must clearly state that *the movement for regime change, including the actions of duped students and others, is an insurrection in support of our colonial bondage.* Those who seek economic justice can only find it in the just, new paradigm of the BRICS and the future it portends. To think otherwise is not mere foolishness, but a case of insane blindness to the world of struggle in which we now live.

The articles to which I refer are these:

• South Africa Bucks British Opposition, Goes Nuclear
• No to British Regime Change in South Africa
• British Drive Against BRICS Member South Africa Intensifies
• Color Revolution Factors Active in South Africa; Zuma Unable To Attend Bandung Summit
• Regime Change Movement, Against BRICS and Nuclear Power, Is 'Marching to Pretoria'